ragamuffin books

If you are enjoying this notebook, please consider leaving a review. We would appreciate it very much.

THIS NOTEBOOK BELONGS TO:

....

Made in the USA
Columbia, SC
06 December 2024

48571810R00062